NICOLAUS

COPERNICUS

FATHER OF MODERN ASTRONOMY

SPECIAL LIVES IN HISTORY THAT BECOME
Signature LIVES

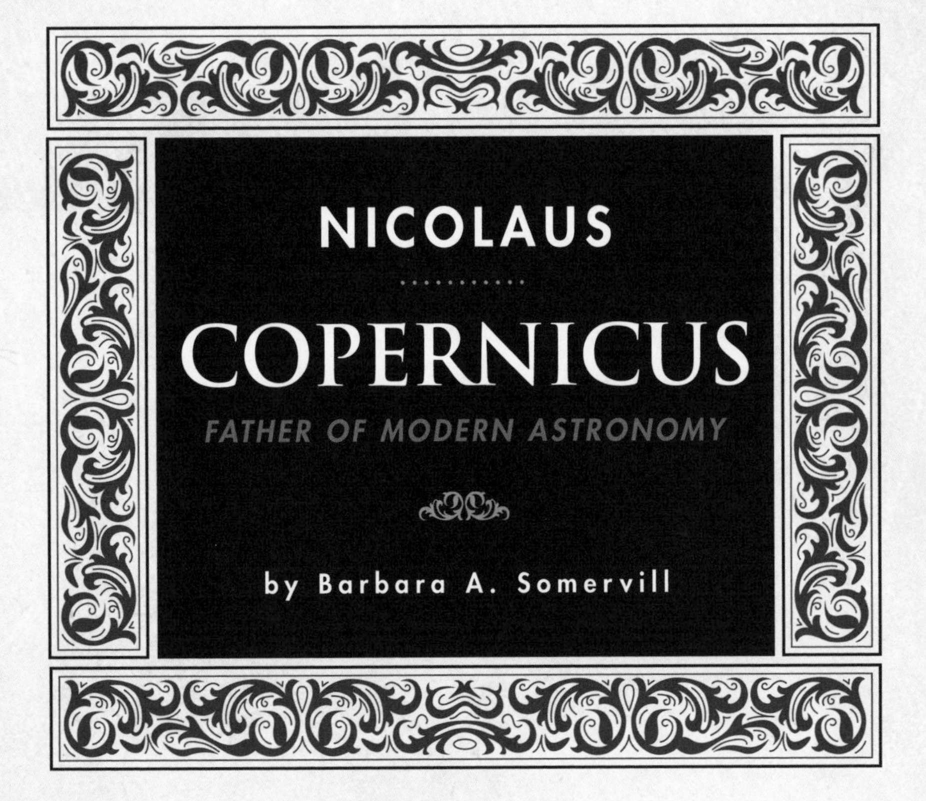

NICOLAUS COPERNICUS

FATHER OF MODERN ASTRONOMY

by Barbara A. Somervill

Content Adviser: Kerry V. Magruder, Ph.D.,
Librarian, History of Science Collections,
and Adjunct Associate Professor,
Department of the History of Science,
University of Oklahoma

Reading Adviser: Rosemary G. Palmer, Ph.D.,
Department of Literacy, College of Education,
Boise State University

COMPASS POINT BOOKS — MINNEAPOLIS, MINNESOTA

Compass Point Books
3109 West 50th Street, #115
Minneapolis, MN 55410

Visit Compass Point Books on the Internet at *www.compasspointbooks.com*
or e-mail your request to *custserv@compasspointbooks.com.*

Editor: Jennifer VanVoorst
Lead Designer: Jaime Martens
Photo Researcher: Svetlana Zhurkina
Page Production: Heather Griffin, Bobbie Nuytten
Cartographer: XNR Productions, Inc.
Educational Consultant: Diane Smolinski

Managing Editor: Catherine Neitge
Art Director: Keith Griffin
Production Director: Keith McCormick
Creative Director: Terri Foley

Library of Congress Cataloging-in-Publication Data
Somervill, Barbara A.
Nicolaus Copernicus: father of modern astronomy / by Barbara A. Somervill.
p. cm. — (Signature lives)
Includes bibliographical references and index.
ISBN-13: 978-0-7565-0812-8 (hardcover)
ISBN-10: 0-7565-0812-6 (hardcover)
ISBN-13: 978-0-7565-1058-9 (paperback)
ISBN-10: 0-7565-1058-9 (paperback)
1. Copernicus, Nicolaus, 1473-1543—Juvenile literature. 2. Astronomers—Poland—Biography—Juvenile literature. I. Title. II. Series.
QB36.C8S64 2005
520'.92—dc22 2004019030

Printed in the United States of America.

Signature Lives

RENAISSANCE ERA

The Renaissance was a cultural movement that started in Italy in the early 1300s. The word *renaissance* comes from a Latin word meaning "rebirth," and during this time, Europe experienced a rebirth of interest and achievement in the arts, science, and global exploration. People reacted against the religion-centered culture of the Middle Ages to find greater value in the human world. By the time the Renaissance came to a close, around 1600, people had come to look at their world in a brand new way.

Nicolaus Copernicus

Table of Contents

NON PAREM PAVLO GRATIĀ REQ
VENIAM PETRI NEQ POSCO, SED
IN CRVCIS LIGNO DEDERAS LATR
SEDVLVS OP

1 The Center of the Universe

Nicolaus Copernicus lay in bed. At 70, he was a very old man for his time. He had already outlived many of his generation, and now he too was dying. A recent stroke had left him paralyzed on his right side, and he slipped in and out of consciousness. Friends stood around his bed, talking softly, waiting for the end to come. In a rare moment of clarity, Copernicus felt someone place something weighty in his hand. It was his book! His life's work sat squarely on his palm. *On the Revolutions of the Heavenly Spheres* finally had been published.

Although Nicolaus Copernicus had spent his professional career as a minor official in the Roman Catholic Church, it was his theories about astronomy—written down in his book—that made up his

A portrait of Nicolaus Copernicus hangs in St. John's Church in Torún, Poland.

real life's work. Copernicus's great passion was the stars, and he had spent his lifetime developing and refining a view of the universe that turned established knowledge on its head.

Sadly, Copernicus died the day he first saw his newly published book. He never knew what a stir his ideas would create in the years to come, or how they would change the course of astronomy forever.

When Nicolaus Copernicus was born in Poland in 1473, Europe was a very different place than it is today. At this time, clergymen of the Roman Catholic Church were often the only people who could read, write, or do arithmetic. Copernicus was a canon at Poland's Frombork Cathedral, and like many people in service to the church, he was an educated man. He spoke Polish, Latin, and Greek. He studied mathematics, astronomy, law, and medicine. He read the ideas of ancient Greek astronomers and mathematicians. These learned men believed Earth was the center of the universe and that all the other heavenly bodies, including the sun, revolved around it. Most people in Copernicus's time—including the church—supported this view of the universe.

Copernicus, however, observed the movement of the stars and planets and performed his own calculations, and he decided that Earth revolved around the sun. The Greeks—and the church—were wrong. In the 1500s, though, defying the church led

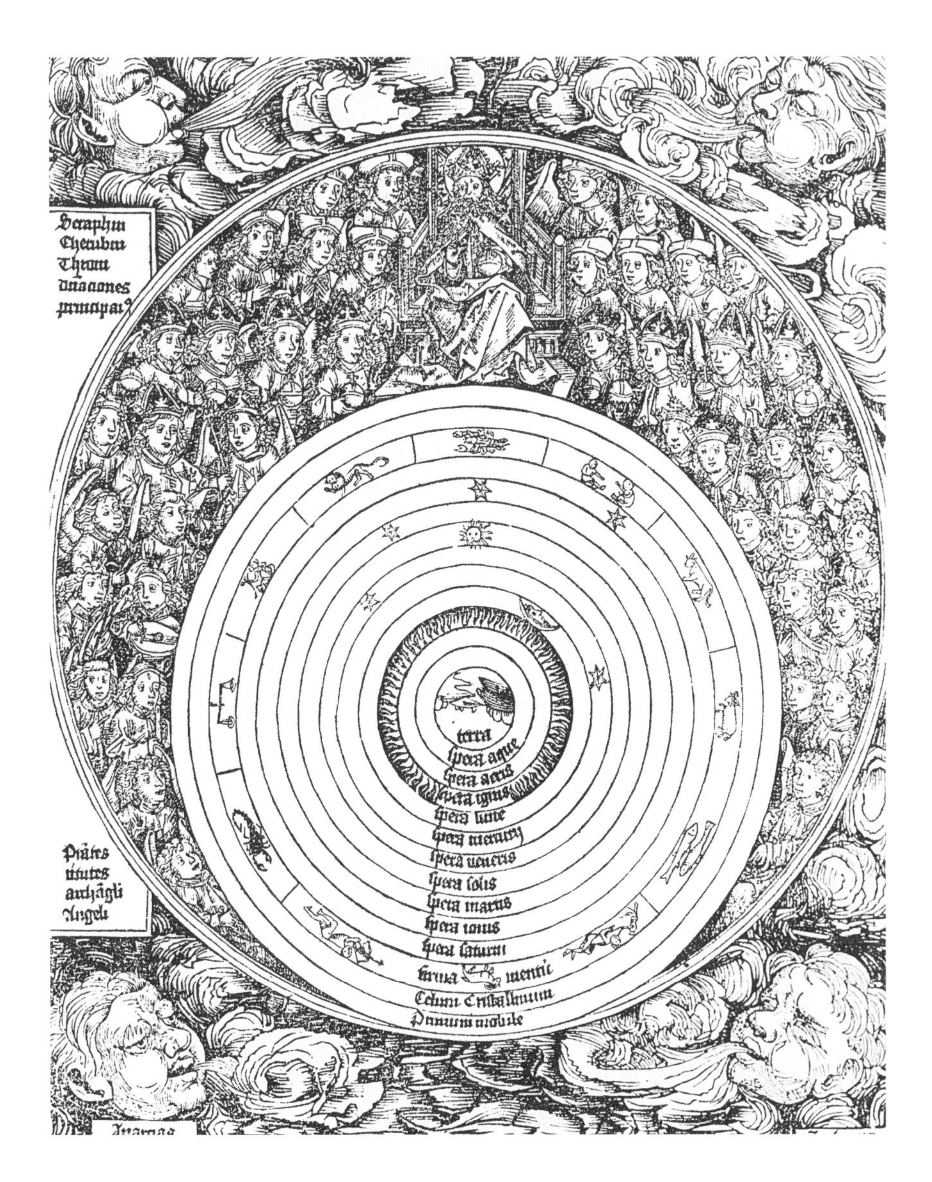

An illustration depicts a view of the universe in which the sun, stars, and planets revolve around Earth.

to serious trouble.

People who disagreed with the church sometimes were tortured. Some were burned at the stake, beheaded, or drawn and quartered, a punishment that ripped a person into pieces. Not many people spoke out against the teachings of the church.

In later years, those who supported Copernicus were tried by the church as heretics. Italian scientist Galileo Galilei was found guilty of "vehement suspicion of heresy" and sentenced to house arrest for life. Printed books by Copernicus, Galileo, and Johannes Kepler appeared on the church's list of banned books, called the Index of Prohibited Books. *The church did not remove those books from the Index until 1835. In 1992, the church finally admitted it treated Galileo badly—more than 300 years after the fact.*

Yet Copernicus did disagree. All his calculations pointed toward a new model of the universe. He also knew that in the fifth century B.C., the Greek mathematician Pythagoras had suggested that Earth moved. He learned that the great astronomer Aristarchus thought the sun was the center of the universe. To him, these ideas made sense.

Between 1514 and 1530, Copernicus wrote six small books explaining his heliocentric, or sun-centered, theories. These books were collected to form one large book, a volume titled *De Revolutionibus Orbium Coelestium*, or *On the Revolutions of the Heavenly Spheres.* In this book, Copernicus explained his theory that the sun was actually the center of the universe and the planets revolved around it. Earth was just another planet circling the sun.

In his work, Copernicus shifted the spotlight

that had shone on man for centuries. The German poet Johann von Goethe wrote in 1808:

> *Of all discoveries and opinions, none may have exerted a greater effect on the human spirit than the doctrine of Copernicus. The world had scarcely become known as round and complete in itself when it was asked to waive the tremendous privilege of being the center of the universe. Never, perhaps, was a greater demand on mankind—for by this admission so many things vanished in mist and smoke.*

Humans were no longer the center of the universe—or even the center of attention. Copernicus's ideas changed the way people thought about the world and themselves. His ideas changed everything.

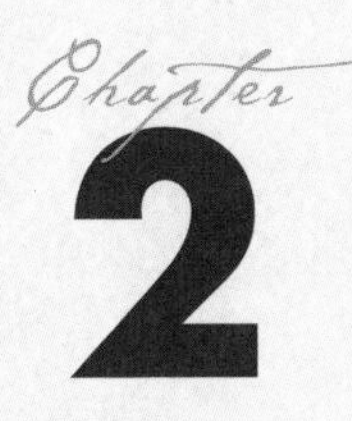

A Childhood in Poland

On February 19, 1473, at about 4:30 in the afternoon, Nicolaus Copernicus was born in Thorn, Poland, now known as Torún, Poland. His name was Nicolaus Koppernigk, but written records show the family name with several different spellings. The most common spellings were Koppernigk and Kopernik. The name was perhaps derived from the word for copper, which Nicolaus's father, also named Nicolaus, bought and sold. Nicolaus's father also served as a judge, a banker, and an alderman on the town council. Nicolaus's mother Barbara was the daughter of a wealthy merchant family, the Watzenrodes. Nicolaus, the youngest of four children, had a brother Andreas, and two sisters, Barbara and Catherina.

A statue of Nicolaus Copernicus stands in his home town of Torún, Poland.

It is unsuaul that we know as much as we do about the birth of Nicolaus Copernicus. Such information was usually not recorded in the 15th century. However, at some point in his life, an astrologer cast Copernicus's horoscope, which requires—and records—the specific date and time of his birth. Copernicus's horoscope emphasized his mathematical and organizational skills—skills that would eventually bring him great renown.

In the 1400s, life in Torún, Poland, depended on the Vistula River. Residents called the city "the Queen of the Vistula." On market days, traders floated rafts downstream from the city of Warsaw, carrying pigs, vegetables, fabric, pots, and pans.

Two walls and a moat surrounded Torún. Guards stood watch from the three towers built into the walls. The towers and walls kept the city's 10,000 residents safe from barbarians, thieves, and rogues.

Attacks on the city happened often. To protect themselves, Torún's men practiced archery. These men formed a marksmen's society, and when the alarm sounded, they grabbed their bows and arrows and scurried up onto Torún's walls, ready for action.

The Koppernigk family lived on Sante Annagasse, or St. Anne Street, in Torún, in a house Barbara Koppernigk's father gave them. It was a small, narrow brick house that opened directly onto the street. The downstairs had a hall and a tiny room. A large living room took up most of the sec-

Nicolaus Copernicus grew up in this house on St. Anne Street, now known as Copernicus Street, in Torún, Poland.

ond floor, where the family met visitors and ate meals. Bedrooms were small and had feather beds, a chest for clothing, and sometimes a chair.

As a boy, Nicolaus had a varied education. He attended a church school, where he learned reading, writing, singing, drawing, and mathematics. School prepared boys for their future, but girls did not go to school unless it was in a convent.

Nicholas learned to use a sword, shoot arrows, and ride a horse. These skills were needed when

In Copernicus's time, Poland was outside of the Holy Roman Empire.

boys became men and helped defend their cities.

In the 15th century, a family's sons usually followed one of three careers. The first son inherited the family business, land, and wealth—if there was any. Other sons either joined the military or the clergy. Girls married or entered a convent to become a nun. The Koppernigk children followed this typical pattern. Andreas and Nicolaus entered into service for the church, Barbara took vows as a nun, and Catherina married a merchant.

When Nicolaus was just 10 years old, his father died at the age of 63, which was considered quite old at that time. Nicolaus's uncle, Lucas Watzenrode, became guardian of the Koppernigk children. Nicolaus and his brothers and sisters still lived with their mother, but their uncle was responsible for the children's future and security.

Watzenrode was a hot-tempered man who came from a wealthy merchant family and enjoyed the power that money offered. He was also a bishop in the Roman Catholic Church, which ran like a business: A man could get rich working for the church, and Watzenrode did. Watzenrode wanted his nephews to enjoy the comfortable lives that the church could provide. First, however, they needed a college education.

A Long-Term Student

In Europe in the late 1400s, dramatic changes were taking place. The Middle Ages gave way to the Renaissance, a rebirth of learning. The University of Kraków, Poland's only college, became a center of education. Bishop Watzenrode had gone to school there, and he sent his nephews to study in Kraków as well.

The University of Kraków was famous for science, philosophy, and mathematics. Students flocked there to study astronomy. The best minds in Poland taught classes—but the classes were open only to men.

For the 1491–1492 school year, the university register reads, "*Nicolaus Nicolai de Thuronia solvit totum*"—or "Nicolaus, son of Nicolaus, from Torún

Nicolaus Copernicus studied many subjects at many universities, but his true interest was always astronomy.

The courtyard of the Old University section of the University of Kraków.

is registered and paid his fees." Bishop Watzenrode wanted Nicolaus and Andreas to study canon law—the laws of the church. Nicolaus, however, studied liberal arts. He took classes in Latin and Greek, read poetry by Virgil and Ovid, and studied mathematics and astronomy. Nicolaus changed his last name to Copernicus, a Latin version of Koppernigk, since Latin was the language used by scholars.

The school year had two terms. The winter term started on October 18; the summer term began on April 15. Classes began at what was called 15 hours, or 8 o'clock in the morning. Class times were based on the number of hours since sunset the day before. Each class lasted four hours.

The professor stood above his students and lectured the entire four hours. Copernicus and his fellow students sat on wooden benches or on the floor, hurriedly taking notes with a quill pen and ink. Afternoons were a time to review what the professor had taught during the morning.

While Copernicus was a student at the University of Kraków, an Italian named Christopher Columbus sailed under the flag of Spain in search of a sea route to the lands known as the Indies. What he found, instead, was a new world not yet known to Renaissance Europe.

Few students owned textbooks. Printing with movable type was relatively new, having been invented just 36 years before in 1455. Not many books had been printed this way yet, and few students could afford the ones that already existed. Instead, students read from textbooks

Copernicus studied in this geometry room at the University of Kraków.

that were available in the school library and made notes on the contents. Textbooks had changed little from one generation to the next. The astronomy text commonly used in most colleges in Copernicus's time was written in the 1200s, and many of the theories were well over 1,000 years old. Copernicus studied the Earth-centered model of the universe of early Greek thinker Ptolemy, which formed the backbone of European developments in astronomy to the 15th century.

Nevertheless, while a student at Kraków, Copernicus was exposed to newer ideas in astronomy, including the theories of Islamic astronomers that increased contact between cultures had recently made known in Europe. He learned the introductory planetary theory of Georg von Peurbach's *Theoricae Novae Planetarum*, or *New Theory of the Planets*, which was published in 1472. Copernicus also studied with Albert Brudzewski, a professor who had been a student of the renowned astronomer Regiomontanus.

In 1476, three years after Copernicus was born, the astronomer Regiomontanus published his Kalendarium, *which predicted the positions of the sun and moon for 40 years on the basis of astronomy updated from the early Greek thinker, Ptolemy. Christopher Columbus took a later German edition of the* Kalendarium *on his fourth voyage to the New World and used its prediction of the 1504 lunar eclipse to frighten his native hosts on the island of Jamaica.*

After attending college for two years, Copernicus and his brother left school. Copernicus did not earn a degree at Kraków, and he hadn't studied church law as his uncle had asked. He was not done with his education, however. He followed a common pattern of European schooling in the late 1400s in which young men often started at one college and then finished at another.

Copernicus's uncle had earned a degree from the University of Bologna in Italy, so he decided to send his nephews there to complete their education. He still intended for them to study canon law, and the University of Bologna was the most highly regarded school of law in the world.

In Copernicus's time, Italy was made up of city-states, which were small republics, and states governed by the pope.

The trip to Bologna was not easy. There were no planes, trains, or cars to speed their travel. In fact, the

brothers walked, traveling over the Alps on foot into Italy. They probably passed through present-day Slovakia, Hungary, and Austria on their way to Bologna in northern Italy.

After about two months of foot travel, the two brothers finally arrived in Bologna, an old, busy, and thriving city. It served as a market center in the foothills of the Apennine Mountains.

Nicolaus and Andreas Copernicus enrolled at the university in January 1497. At that time, the University of Bologna, founded in 1119, was more than 300 years old and attracted students and professors throughout Europe. Its students came from Prussia, Germany, Denmark, Lithuania, Belgium, Hungary, and Sweden. Although this time Copernicus did study canon law, he also studied mathematics and astronomy. In particular, he studied with astronomer Dominico Maria di Novara, with whom he made his first recorded observation of the stars.

Bishop Watzenrode wanted Copernicus to have a secure income, and he put pressure on the church to elect his nephew as a canon, a clergyman who worked for the church but was not a priest. Canons usually lived in a cathedral and ran the business of the church, doing just about any job that the church needed done. Their positions were for life, and when one canon died, a new one was elected to replace him. A canon's yearly salary was just under 100 marks—equal to a doctor's salary at that time.

In October 1497, Copernicus became a canon of Warmia, a district in Poland. However, he was allowed to study for a few more years before officially beginning his duties.

In 1500, the Roman Catholic Church was celebrating an important anniversary, and Pope Alexander VI asked all faithful Catholics to come to Rome for the festivities. Copernicus, who was only a few hundred miles away in Bologna, joined more than 200,000 pilgrims heading to Rome. In Rome, Copernicus gave lectures on math and took part in church events, but his most remarkable experience had nothing to do with either mathematics or the church. On November 6, 1500, Copernicus witnessed a lunar eclipse, as the shadow of Earth passed over the moon. For him, this was a monumental event. He later would compare that eclipse with others, helping confirm the new view of the universe he was developing even then.

Copernicus's chapter, the organization that governed canons, decided that having a doctor in the group would be handy. So, Copernicus changed his course of study again—and his school. This time, he studied medicine at the University of Padua, a well-known center of medical learning. Besides, Lucas Watzenrode wanted Copernicus to go, and few clergymen stood up against Bishop Watzenrode.

Copernicus's interest in astronomy grew when he observed a lunar eclipse.

Copernicus found that his knowledge of astronomy, which was his primary interest, helped him as a medical student. Educated people of the time believed that a planetary influence might affect the course of a disease. Doctors relied on their ability to predict the positions of planets at different times of the year. They used mathematical astronomy to help determine when to give medicines or follow other medical procedures.

Physicians of this time relied primarily on herbal remedies to treat illnesses. Doctors would make medicines from strange ingredients, like ground animal horns and gems. Copernicus's class notes from his time as a medical student show a view of the medicines available and the diseases they treated:

> *An infusion of the roots of tamarisk on the pustules [blisters] helps treat leprosy. … The juice from oak … helps treat … ulcers. … Take resin from a fruit tree, boil it in beer three times, and drink with meals, helps treat podagra [a swollen big toe].*

To most of his remedies, Copernicus also added, "God willing, the medicament [remedy] will help."

After three years in Padua, Copernicus changed schools again. He resumed his studies in canon law at the University of Ferrara, north of Bologna. At this time, students paid for their degrees as well as for their classes. Many students took classes at one university but then bought their degrees from a cheaper school. A degree from the University of Ferrara only cost 25 ducats, much less than a degree from the University of Padua. Perhaps this is the reason Copernicus decided to switch to the University of Ferrara.

Copernicus may also have heard of the teachings of Celio Calcagnini, a professor of astronomy at the University of Ferrara. Calcagnini broke with the

An illustration from an early 16th-century medical book shows bloodletting and skin disease treatment.

commonly held view of the universe and taught that Earth moved. Calcagnini's teaching might have intrigued Copernicus and prompted him to leave Padua for Ferrara.

Regardless of his motive, Copernicus continued his studies at the University of Ferrara and received his degree in canon law on May 31, 1503. He was 30 years old. It was time to return to Poland and begin his work for the church.

Chapter

4 In Service to the Church

When Copernicus returned to Poland, he met with an unexpected surprise. Instead of beginning his work as a canon, he was sent to live with his uncle. Bishop Lucas Watzenrode lived in Heilsberg Castle, in the province of Warmia, Poland. Copernicus went to work there as the bishop's secretary, and although he did not have a medical degree, he became the bishop's personal physician.

Castle life at Heilsberg was similar to life in other European royal castles of the early 1500s. Heilsberg Castle was self-sufficient. A kitchen garden provided onions, turnips, and other vegetables. Orchards grew apples, pears, and other fruit. An herb garden produced seasoning for food and remedies for illnesses. A dairy provided milk and cheese,

In this portrait, Copernicus is shown holding a lily of the valley, a flower that was a symbol of the medical profession.

Heilsberg Castle was the home of Lucas Watzenrode, bishop of Warmia.

and herds of pigs and sheep provided meat on the table. Men also hunted and fished. The castle probably had a brewery for making beer or ale and a separate winery. Several hundred people lived and worked in the castle, and Copernicus was just one worker among many.

Copernicus enjoyed a life of relative luxury at his uncle's home. He had few responsibilities and continued studying astronomy and mathematics. He began to develop and refine his ideas about the organization of the universe and the movement of Earth.

At this time, the Roman Catholic Church held the view that Earth was the center of the universe. This seemed obvious to church scholars because the sun, moon, and stars appeared to move around Earth. In the 12th century, Peter Lombard of the University of Paris described the Roman Catholic viewpoint when he said:

> *Just as man is made for the sake of God ... so the universe is made for the sake of man. ... Therefore, is man placed at the middle point of the universe, that he may both serve and be served.*

The church's view of the universe was supported by Earth-centered models created by early Greek thinkers such as Ptolemy, Aristotle, and Archimedes.

Copernicus, however, held a different view. While caring for the Bishop Watzenrode's health, he began writing a booklet titled *Commentariolus*, or *Little Commentary.* The booklet presented Copernicus's early ideas about how planets moved in the universe. In *Little Commentary*, Copernicus wrote that Earth

Although his primary interest continued to be astronomy, while at Heilsberg, Copernicus found time to indulge other interests as well. He enjoyed painting and translating poetry. In 1509, he published his first book, a Latin translation of the Greek letters of seventh-century writer Theophylactus. This was the first Greek-to-Latin translation ever published in Poland.

A geocentric, or Earth-centered, view of the universe is based on the theories of the Greek philosopher Aristotle.

spun on its own axis as it traveled around the sun. This was groundbreaking thinking.

Copernicus wrote:

> *I began to consider the mobility [movement] of the Earth and even though the idea seemed absurd, nevertheless, I knew that others before me had been granted the freedom to imagine any circles whatsoever for explaining the heavenly phenomena.*

These early ideas became the foundation of Copernicus's theories of a sun-centered universe.

Earthly events, however, took Copernicus's time away from studying the heavens. His brother, Andreas, suffered from leprosy. Known today as Hansen's disease, leprosy is an ongoing infection that affects the skin, eyes, nose, and nerve endings, and can cause crippling deformities. In 1508, Andreas left his brother and Poland behind to return to Italy, the center of advanced medicine at the time, where he eventually died from the disease in about 1518.

A treatment for leprosy was found in the 1940s, but in Copernicus's time, sufferers went to live in leper colonies. There, they lived an isolated life as their bodies rotted from the disease until they died.

In 1512, Bishop Lucas Watzenrode died, and Copernicus's job came to an end. It was time for him to go to Frombork, Poland, and assume his duties as a canon.

The city of Frombork, in the province of Warmia, was founded in about 1278. During the 1300s, the city leaders erected stone walls to protect Frombork from attackers. Two main gates—the Windmill Gate and the Blacksmith's Gate—allowed visitors to enter the city. On market days, farmers, tanners, fishermen, weavers, and other vendors poured through the gates to set up stalls and sell their goods. The center of life was the cathedral, and this cathedral became Nicolaus Copernicus's home.

Copernicus lived a comfortable life in an

As a canon in Frombork, Poland, Copernicus lived at the cathedral.

apartment on the cathedral grounds. He had his own living room, study, bedroom, and small kitchen, but he shared general rooms such as halls, meeting rooms, chapels, and dining halls with members of his chapter. A woman was hired to clean, cook, and do his laundry. Best of all, he was allowed to pursue his own interests, as long as he did his job.

The name for the women who were hired to do the canons' household chores was focaria, *which meant both housekeeper and mistress. In the 1500s, clergymen sometimes had relationships with women. Copernicus's* focaria, *Anna Schilling, was both his housekeeper and his companion.*

Copernicus had a varied background and was skilled in many areas. As a result, the chapter gave Copernicus a variety of jobs. One of his first jobs was as a mapmaker. At that time, mapmaking was recognized as a branch of mathematics; the ancient Greek astronomer Ptolemy himself had pioneered mathematical methods of mapmaking. Copernicus's job was to draw an accurate map of Warmia and the borders it shared with Prussia. Maps were scarce at the time, and accurate ones were even rarer, but Copernicus applied his knowledge of math and science to his mapmaking. Between 1510 and 1512, he created a map of Warmia that was so accurate that the Knights of the Teutonic Order, a German group of militant monks, tried to steal it. They wanted to know the quickest routes between one city and the next, so they could loot a town and then escape along a safe route.

In addition to his duties as a mapmaker, Copernicus also held two other jobs—bursar and chancellor. As the bursar, he was in charge of the chapter's money. He ordered goods, paid bills, and collected fees or taxes on chapter property. As the chancellor, he served as the chapter's secretary, recording deeds, letters, and other business. Copernicus also recorded leases and rental terms and collected rents, which were paid in bushels of wheat, chickens, pigs, and so on.

After four years, the chapter relieved Copernicus of both his jobs, although he continued mapmaking until 1529. His new freedom allowed him to buy a house in Frombork and set up a makeshift astronomical observatory in the attic.

At this time, the Roman Catholic Church was dealing with a major problem. Europeans and the Catholic Church followed a calendar that had been put in place in about 45 B.C., but the calendar was incorrect. The problem with this calendar, called the Julian calendar, was that a year did not equal an even number of days, which made for a messy calendar at the end of the year.

Under the Julian calendar, a year had 365 days divided into 12 months. Every fourth year, there was a leap year with an extra day. However, that leap day didn't completely smooth things out. Over the centuries, the calendar got farther and farther off target, until by Copernicus's time it was off by 10 days.

As a result, the church had a hard time figuring out when Easter should be scheduled. In 1513, Pope Leo X asked leaders of every country in the Holy Roman Empire—most of Europe at the time—to send their best scholars to Rome.

The Julian calendar was named after Julius Caesar, during whose reign as emperor of the Roman Empire it was created.

In 1516, Copernicus was asked to help with the calendar problem, but he stayed in Poland instead of

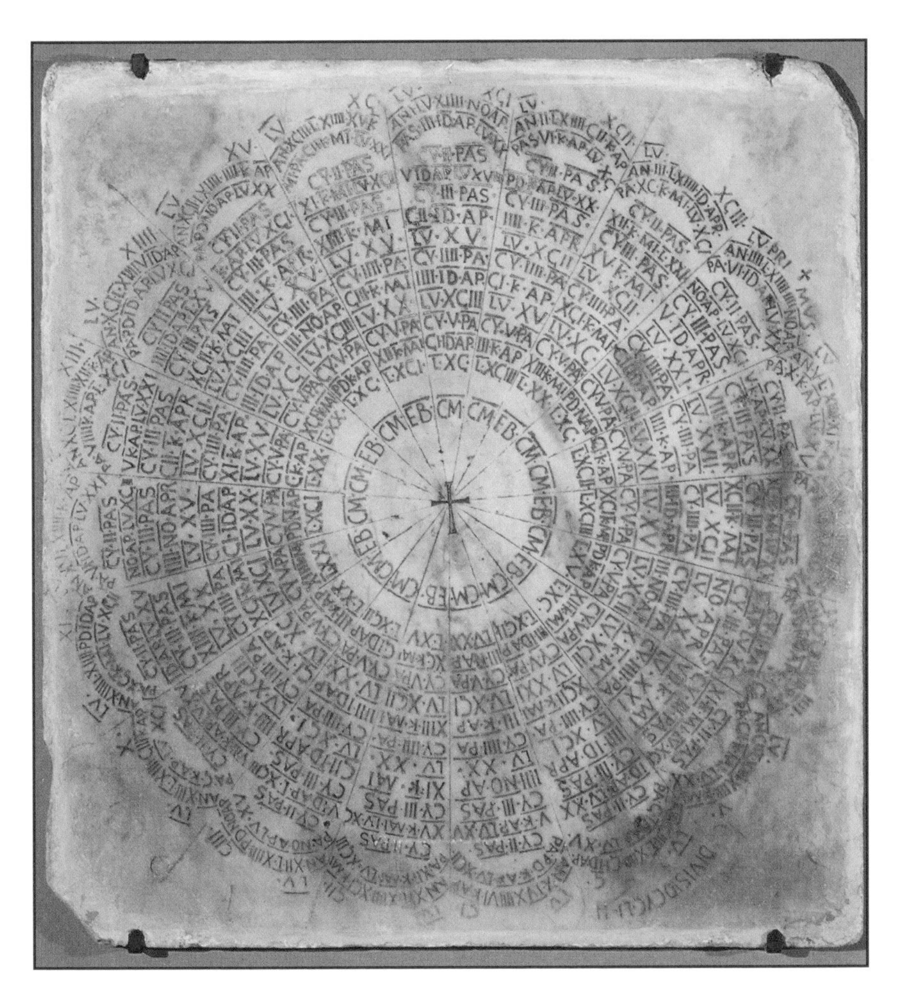

attending the council in Rome. He said:

> *I have devoted my attention in investigating [the length of the year] and in particular in 1515 A.D. I found 186 days, 5 1/2 day-minutes are completed between with vernal [spring] and autumnal [fall] equinoxes.*

Copernicus computed the number of days in the year at 365.2425 days—not far off from the actual number of days accepted today. However, he decided that the calendar should not be adjusted until more observations and calculations were made. The problems with the calendar were not solved until 1582, when the Gregorian calendar was introduced. That calendar, named for Pope Gregory XIII, is the calendar we use today.

Having put aside the calendar issue, Copernicus turned his mind to the task of coining money. In the early 1500s, gold poured into Europe from the New World and Africa. Every king, duke, and count—and anyone else who wanted to—minted coins, which varied in value, weight, and metal content. No one could figure out what the money in their pockets was actually worth. Copernicus devised a table that listed common coins and their values. By using Copernicus's table, people knew the value of their money.

Around this time, the Roman Catholic Church came under attack. In 1517, Martin Luther, a German priest, nailed his *Ninety-five Theses* to the door of the church of Wittenberg, Germany. Luther wanted the church to change its practices and end dishonesty within the church. He also disagreed with the

Catholic priest Martin Luther started the movement known as the Protestant Reformation.

unquestioned power of the pope. Luther's rebellion was only the beginning. Soon small groups of reformers started their own churches. Because they were protesting Catholic practices and seeking to reform the church, their movement came to be known as the Protestant Reformation.

In 1519, the attack on the Roman Catholic Church in Poland changed from words to deeds. The Knights of the Teutonic Order brought war to Poland as they rampaged through the land. The Knights were not interested in church reform. They wanted church money, land, and power.

The Teutonic Order had begun in the 1100s as a military order that provided hospitals for sick travelers. Later, the knights swarmed over Central Europe to convert the resident barbarians to Christianity. They brought the word of Jesus Christ on the tip of their swords.

By the 1400s, most Europeans had been converted to Christianity, and about 90 percent of them followed the Roman Catholic Church. Since there was no need for converting barbarians anymore, the knights sought to gain power, as they stormed through towns and cities, taking valuable land. They became an on-land version of pirates.

In 1519, these Teutonic Knights swept through the region where Nicolaus Copernicus lived. When it became obvious they were headed toward

Frombork, Copernicus wrote to Poland's King Sigismund for help:

> *We ourselves are not sufficiently safeguarded to repel ... an attack and we fear lest the enemy, who is already so near, should besiege us also. Therefore, we humbly appeal to Your Holy Majesty to come to our aid as quickly as possible.*

The knights intercepted the letter and prevented

The chief fortress of the Teutonic Knights sits on the Nogat River in Malbork, Poland.

The Holy Roman Empire, based in German-speaking areas of central Europe, existed for nearly a millennium—from 843 to 1806. It was closely associated with the Roman Catholic Church. However, by the time of Copernicus, the empire had fallen into decline as lesser kings and dukes asserted their independence. Copernicus lived in Warmia, a Polish region loyal to the king of Poland. The Teutonic Knights, loyal to the emperor, ruled Polish lands east of Warmia, and looked to gain more territory to the west. So, in his defense of Frombork, Copernicus was working to protect not only the physical buildings of his town but also the very existence of the independent country of Poland.

it from reaching King Sigismund. They entered Frombork and attacked and burned much of the city. They took large tracts of land from the chapter.

A few months later, the war ended, and peace was declared. Nicolaus Copernicus negotiated the return of lands to the church, and helped with the massive chore of rebuilding Frombork from the ashes up.

For the next several years, Copernicus served the chapter in a variety of jobs. He became chancellor again and represented the chapter at regional church and political meetings. He inspected the new defenses built to protect Frombork and supervised the writing and settlement of wills.

Yet, throughout all this time, Copernicus had one passion and one goal. He was, first and foremost, an astronomer. He set up an observatory on top of a cathedral tower to observe the skies,

Copernicus studied the skies from his observatory in Frombork, Poland.

measure angles, and compute distances. He mapped the movement of the planets and realized the early models he had studied in school did not explain the results of his calculations. Could these early theories be incorrect? As Copernicus collected and analyzed the new information, bit by bit, he put together a brand new vision of the universe.

ARISTOTELI STAGIRITAE

Chapter 5 Look to the Stars

Copernicus, who had studied the great astronomers of the past, was familiar with the ideas of Aristarchus, Archimedes, Ptolemy, and Aristotle. Much of the work of these early scientists involved geometry. As a mathematician, he appreciated the theories of these Greek scientists.

The astronomy Copernicus had studied in college was based on the ideas of Claudius Ptolemaeus, known as Ptolemy, who lived in the second century A.D.—about 1,400 years before Copernicus. Ptolemy, an astronomer, geographer, and mathematician, lived in Alexandria, Egypt, a center of learning in the ancient world. He prepared a calendar in which he predicted weather and plotted the positions of the morning and evening stars. During

The Greek philosopher Aristotle is shown here in a painting by Joos van Ghent.

his life, Ptolemy catalogued 1,022 stars.

Ptolemy wrote *Megalë Syntaxis tes Astronomias*, better known as the *Almagest ("The Greatest")*. He described a tidy system of stars, planets, sun, and moon that all revolved around Earth. The *Almagest* included 13 sections that noted the position of the stars and offered models of planetary motion.

Ptolemy believed Earth was the center of everything, Earth did not move, and everything else moved around Earth.

Aristarchus of Samos was also discussed in Copernicus's time. Born in 270 B.C., Aristarchus believed the stars and sun were in fixed positions in the sky. However, he also believed Earth moved around the sun in a circle. This was a new and unusual idea at the time. Aristarchus's ideas, however, were largely ignored.

Archimedes (287–212 B.C.)

Archimedes (287–212 B.C.), a mathematician and inventor, is best known today for his theory of water displacement—that a body put in water loses weight equal to the weight of the water lost. According to legend, Archimedes discovered this when he sank into his bath and the water overflowed. He jumped up and shouted, "Eureka!" which means "I have found it!"

When it came to astronomy, Archimedes contributed two ideas. The first was that the moon's diameter was smaller than Earth's diameter. The second was that Aristarchus's sun-centered model of the universe was wrong. Because most people liked the Earth-centered, or geocentric theory, of the universe, they agreed with Archimedes.

In Copernicus's time, there were two different branches of science that dealt with the universe—astronomy and cosmology. Astronomy was a branch of mathematics that dealt with the mathematical models necessary to predict celestial motions. Cosmology was a branch of physics that dealt with the physical structure of the universe. The models of the universe discussed in Copernicus's time came from both branches. Ptolemy was an astronomer. Aristotle was a cosmologist. Copernicus himself was a mathematical astronomer—not a cosmologist.

Finally, there was Aristotle's model of the universe. Aristotle (384–322 B.C.) lived before Aristarchus, Archimedes, and Ptolemy. It was Aristotle's model that Copernicus identified as wrong. Aristotle believed there were many spheres circling Earth. He also thought Earth was at the center of the universe. Aristotle's model, along with Ptolemy's *Almagest*, was still studied in universities when Copernicus was a student.

Copernicus considered the

Another common reference for Renaissance astronomers was the Alfonsine Tables. *Alfonso X was king of Leon and Castile, two regions of present-day Spain. King Alfonso decided to have scientists compute the positions and movements of the planets. Alfonso had about 50 astronomers working full time on this project. It was completed in 1252.*

complicated maze of spheres and their paths that Aristotle and others had proposed and described such models like this:

> *... they are in exactly the same fix as someone taking from different places hands, feet, head, and the other limbs—shaped very beautifully but not with reference to one body and without correspondence to one another—so that such parts made up a monster rather than a man.*

So, when Copernicus began his studies, the study of astronomy was based on one model of the universe that was about 1,800 years old and constantly being added to. It also was based on two theories by Greeks who had been dead about 1,700 years when Copernicus was born, and a book written 1,400 years earlier, as well as the *Alfonsine Tables*, a reference source about 250 years old.

Except for Aristarchus's model, the prevailing theories all put Earth as the center of the universe. Although among astronomers there was a continuous tradition of discussion and debate, for most of the population, the view remained unquestioned

An illustration shows the Greek mythological figure Atlas supporting a Ptolemaic universe.

for many centuries.

Although Copernicus used more advanced instruments to make his observations and measurements than the early Greeks did, astronomy of the early 1500s was still very different from the tele-

The telescope would not be invented until 1608, when it first appeared in Holland as a novelty device. Later that same year, Galileo Galilei, a supporter of Copernicus's theories, refined the telescope and became the first person to use the new instrument to study the skies. What Galileo viewed with his new instrument supported the findings of Copernicus and made him a believer in a sun-centered model of the universe.

scope-viewing science of today. In Copernicus's time, there were no telescopes—they hadn't been invented yet. Observation of stars, planets, and comets came from the naked eye and some instruments of varying usefulness and accuracy. There were no computers or calculators. All math computations were done with brainpower.

Copernicus used a number of astronomical instruments in his work, including the astrolabe, the Jacob's staff, the triquetrum, and the quadrant.

The astrolabe was originally designed by Ptolemy and later improved by Islamic astronomers. A basic astrolabe consists of a metal disc mounted on a metal circle.

The astrolabe was used in a vertical position. The front could be used to tell the time of day and predict sunrises and sunsets. At sea, astrolabes helped sailors figure out where they were in the open ocean. Ship's navigators and astronomers used astrolabes to measure the angle of stars and planets above the horizon. Astrolabes combined star charts

This astrolabe was used at the University of Kraków when Copernicus was a student.

with a calendar. They were used until the invention of the sextant, a more accurate instrument for determining location at sea.

The Jacob's staff, also called a cross staff, was a simple astronomical invention consisting of two sticks. The longer stick was placed perpendicular to the ground. The shorter stick, a crosspiece, was aimed at the star being measured. A Jacob's staff gave the angle between two distant objects. History records use of a Jacob's staff as early as 284 B.C. Aristarchus used a Jacob's staff to calculate the distance between the sun and Earth. His result was off by several hundred million miles, which shows the accuracy of the Jacob's staff—or of Aristarchus's math.

The sextant, which replaced the astrolabe and quadrant, also measures the angular distance between any two points. Within the frame of a sextant is a movable arm, two mirrors, and a small telescope. The sextant was developed in 1628 and was the primary navigation tool on ships and aircraft until the mid-1900s, when tools such as radar began to replace the sextant.

A triquetrum was like a complex Jacob's staff. It had three hinged rods that could be pointed at distant objects. The triquetrum measured the angular altitude of stars and planets. Historians know that Copernicus used a triquetrum because he built one. Copernicus's triquetrum was 8 feet (2.4 meters) long—a large instrument that was probably rather unwieldy to use.

A quadrant was used to measure angles between two distant bodies. The instrument was used

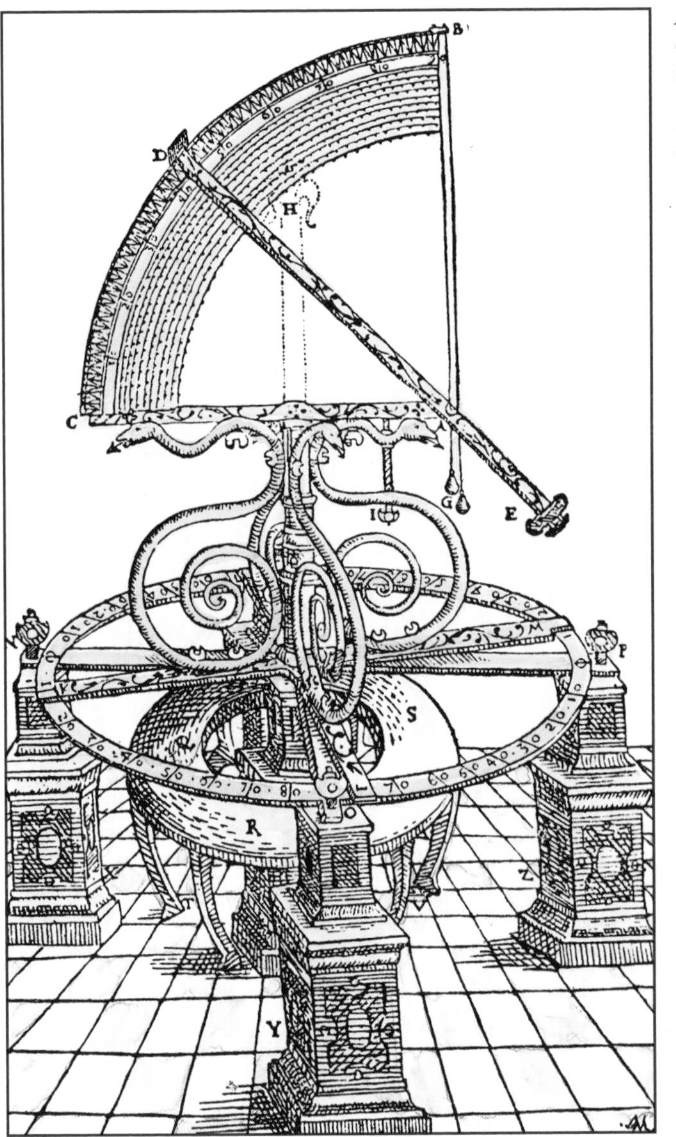

An illustration of a quadrant that belonged to Tycho Brahe, a later supporter of Copernicus

to survey land or to navigate the seas. In the heavens, it measured angles between stars and planets. Quadrant means "one-fourth," a quarter-circle, or

90°. Islamic astronomers invented the quadrant, which consisted of a metal quarter-circle and a movable arm. The user dropped a plumb line perpendicular to the ground. The quadrant was aimed

Some of Copernicus's instruments are on display in his observatory in Frombork Cathedral.

at one object; the arm was aimed at another. The result was the angle formed between the two. Like the astrolabe, the quadrant became obsolete when the sextant was invented in 1628.

Armed with theories and instruments that were centuries old, Copernicus continued to study the universe. He made observations and performed calculations. He compared his findings to the models that were known and accepted. In doing so, he developed a theory that moved people toward a new view of their place in the universe.

IVPITER
Jovis Circulus
GLOBI SVBLVNARIS CVM LVNA ET QVATVOR ELEMENTIS

The Copernican Theory

Copernicus introduced his theories in a small way with *Little Commentary*, a small book he distributed among his friends. In the book, he stated the foundation for what was to be his greater work, *De Revolutionibus Orbium Coelestium*, or *On the Revolutions of the Heavenly Spheres*. In *Little Commentary*, he presented seven basic ideas:

- The distance from Earth to the sun is small compared to the distance from Earth to the stars.
- Earth's center is not the center of the universe.
- The universe has no single center.
- The center of our universe is close to the sun.
- Earth rotates on an axis that makes

An illustration from the 17th-century celestial atlas of Andreas Cellarius shows Nicolaus Copernicus seated beside a map of the Copernican system.

the stars look like they are moving.

- Changes in the sun's position as it relates to Earth happen because of Earth's movement—not the movement of the sun.
- Planets sometimes appear to move backwards because the observers are on Earth, which is

A page from Copernicus's manuscript shows the position of planets in relation to the sun.

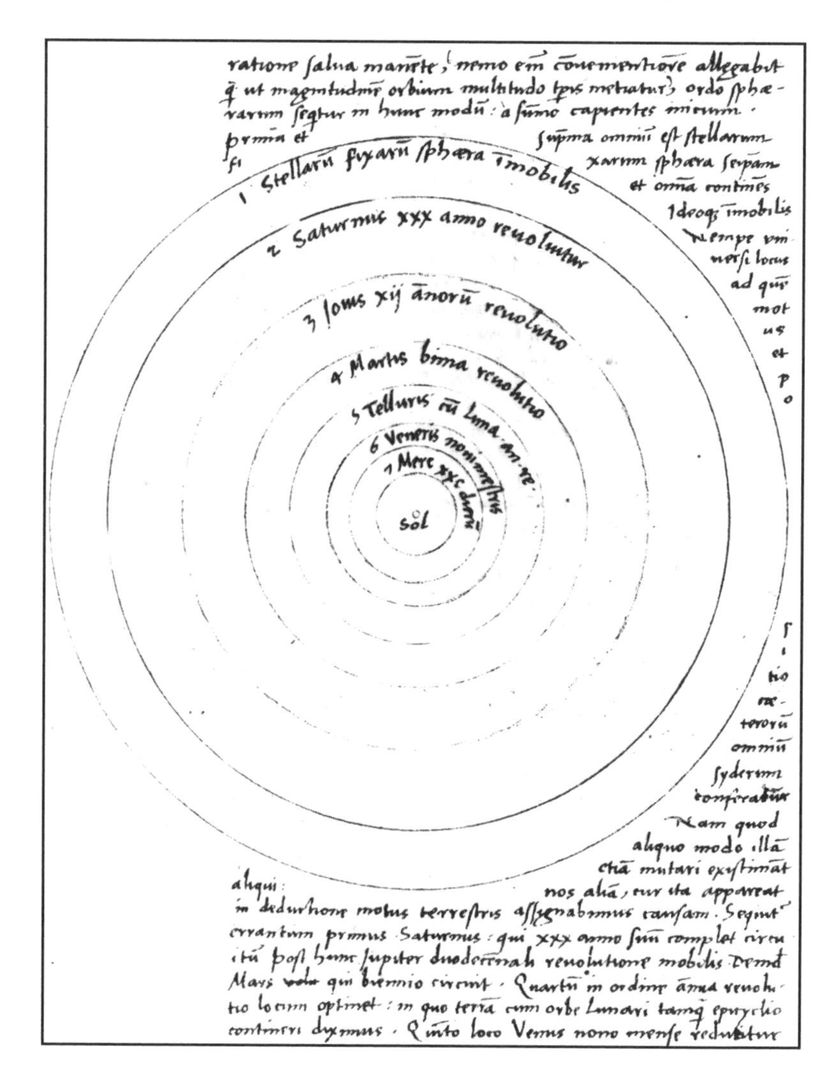

moving forward in its orbit.

Shortly after finishing *Little Commentary*, Copernicus began writing *On the Revolutions*. The year was 1514, and Copernicus would spend more than 16 years writing the six sections that make up the book.

Copernicus opened *On the Revolutions* with a warning: "Let no one untrained in geometry enter here." He wasn't kidding. The book, full of formulas, diagrams, and geometric calculations, explained the motions of planets and "fixed" stars. Much of the writing and math were based on Ptolemy's earlier work, the *Almagest*.

Although Copernicus argued against the commonly held Ptolemaic view of the universe, he relied heavily on Ptolemy's work. In fact, one of the highest compliments astronomers of his own century paid him was to call him "the Ptolemy of our time."

In his book, Copernicus debated the value of physics—known at the time as "natural philosophy"—versus mathematics. When it came to astronomy, he believed mathematics provided true answers, and physics had no basis in fact. He said:

> *I began to be annoyed that the movements of the world machine, created for our sake by the best and most systematic Artisan of all [God], were not understood with greater certainty by the philosophers, who*

otherwise examined so precisely the most insignificant trifles of the world.

In the first section of *On the Revolutions*, Copernicus described the shape of the universe and Earth, and the order of the planets. The idea of a flat Earth had been debunked some time ago, so telling people Earth was round wasn't big news. Copernicus went on to explain that, like Earth, "the universe is spherical … of all forms, the sphere is the most perfect … [and] the sun, moon, planets and stars, are seen to be of this shape." He also explained how to measure the universe.

To help the reader, Copernicus provided a diagram of the universe. The outer layer of the diagram showed a perfect circle that contained all the fixed stars. Just inside the stars was Saturn. Copernicus calculated that Saturn made one revolution of the sun in 30 years. At the third level, Copernicus put Jupiter, with a 12-year revolution. Following Jupiter were Mars, Earth, Venus, and Mercury. He wrote:

Finally, we shall place the Sun himself at the center of the Universe. All this is suggested by the systematic procession of events and the harmony of the whole Universe, if only we face the facts, as they say, 'with both eyes open.'

Copernicus charted the paths of the known planets.

There are some obvious problems with Copernicus's model. However, at the time, it was revolutionary thinking. Today, thanks to advanced telescopes, we know there are other planets in our solar system. And we know that the path of a planet is an ellipse, not a circle.

For observations done with the naked eye and calculations made by hand, Copernicus came to some remarkably accurate conclusions. He set Mercury's "year" at 80 earth days; it actually equals

88 days. He was off on Saturn by about half an earth year and Jupiter by about a month and a half. That's very close calculating.

The second section of his book dealt with the major circles of the globe—the equator, the Tropic of Cancer, the Tropic of Capricorn, and other lines of latitude. Latitude was easy to figure out based on the height of the sun and stars against the horizon. Copernicus offered formulas that would help determine the sunrise and sunset at different latitudes.

In the third section, Copernicus studied equinoxes

A 17th-century illustration shows a Copernican sun-centered world system.

and solstices. An equinox occurs when the sun's position in the sky crosses the equator. On the equinox, day and night both last 12 hours. This happens twice each year—on March 21 and September 23. A solstice occurs when the sun is farthest from the equator. The solstice occurs on December 22 and June 22. December 22 marks the shortest day of the year, and June 22 is the longest day. Copernicus pointed out that equinoxes and solstices were uniform events that occurred at regular intervals.

In the book's fourth section, Copernicus addressed the issue of the moon. He suggested formulas for measuring the size, orbit, and motion of the moon. He also computed the moon's distance from Earth.

Sections five and six dealt with the planets, their orbits, movements, and paths. Copernicus computed each planet's distance from Earth, from each other, and from the sun. He then established various latitudes, like the equator or the Tropic of Cancer, for other

In his preface to On the Revolutions, *Copernicus compared the center of the universe to the center of a temple, fit only for a lamp such as the sun: "Behold, in the middle of the universe resides the Sun. For who, in this most beautiful Temple, would set this lamp in another or a better place, whence to illumine all things at once? For aptly indeed do some call him the lantern ... Truly indeed does the Sun, as if seated upon a royal throne, govern his family of planets as they circle about him."*

planets. While these calculations were not particularly accurate, they were based on sound principles of geometry.

During the years when Copernicus was madly figuring, observing, and recording his theory, he discussed his ideas with other scientists. In one account, Martin Luther, the Protestant reformer, heard rumors about the sun-centered theory Copernicus was developing and immediately dismissed it. Luther was perhaps referring to Copernicus when he said:

Although Martin Luther rejected the Roman Catholic Church, he continued to believe its views on the universe. Nevertheless, Lutherans—the religious group that arose from Luther's split from the Roman Catholic Church—ultimately became the some of the leading defenders of Copernicus in the 16th century.

> *[The] new astrologer ... would prove that the earth moves, not the sky and the firmament, sun and moon. ... The fool would like to reverse the whole art of astronomy! But it says in the Holy Writ that Joshua bade the sun stand still, not the earth.*

For the most part, Copernicus completed *On the Revolutions* in about 1530, but he did not print the book. He was not concerned with what the church might say about his novel theory, but he was a perfectionist. Even after working on his theories for

30 years, he still did not believe that the complete work was ready for publication. As far as he was concerned, there were always more calculations to be checked and rechecked. Besides, most astronomers chose to believe in an Earth-centered universe. The church preferred that belief, too. And Copernicus was a shy, quiet man. He did not welcome the attention that would come with publishing his book.

The public would have to wait until after he died to learn about Copernicus's astounding ideas. Even then, the vast majority of Europeans at the time could not read, and those who could most likely would not understand the math or science in the book. *On the Revolutions* was not destined to become a best seller.

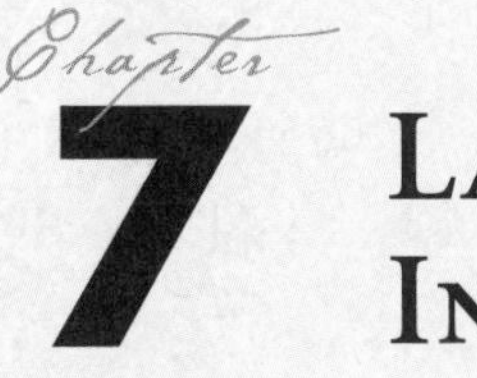

Chapter 7 Late In Life

By the time Copernicus finished writing *On the Revolutions*, he was 57 years old. That is not old today, but the life expectancy of a European man in the 1500s was 30 to 40 years old. People did not have the advantages of central heat, sanitary plumbing, and refrigeration to keep food from spoiling. They didn't have good dental care, medical care, or antibiotics to fight off infections. Smallpox, diphtheria, tuberculosis, and bubonic plague—diseases that are rare today—ran rampant throughout Europe. So, 57 was a ripe, old age.

Late in life, Copernicus continued to revise his book, study the stars, and work for his chapter. In 1531, he was again put in charge of the chapter's money, a job he took very seriously.

After completing the initial writing of On the Revolutions, *Copernicus continued to study the skies.*

Copernicus's original manuscript of On the Revolutions *was lost to the world until the mid-19th century when it was discovered in Prague. The manuscript shows that Copernicus made revision after revision to the text.*

Copernicus immediately addressed the cost of bread—a staple food served at every meal. Bread was costing the chapter too much money, so Copernicus investigated the cost of flour, the other ingredients needed, and the bakers' fees. According to his calculations, bread should have cost the chapter a certain sum, but it did not. Copernicus devised a mathematical table for computing the cost of bread per loaf. The chapter paid only what Copernicus declared was a fair price.

That same year, Copernicus's lifestyle came under criticism. He lived in a house in town, not in Frombork's cathedral. He allowed women to visit him in his home, which angered some clergy members. He agreed to stop having female guests, and said, "I shall so order my affairs that nobody will have any proper pretext to suspect evil of me hereafter." But "women problems" continued to haunt Copernicus.

In 1537, Warmia got a new bishop, Dantiscus, who discovered that Copernicus had a relationship with his housekeeper, Anna Schilling. Bishop Dantiscus ordered Copernicus to send Anna away.

Copernicus lived in this house in town, rather than in Frombork Cathedral.

Now in his 60s, Copernicus was unwilling to change his lifestyle. Besides, Anna refused to leave. This issue was never resolved, and Bishop Dantiscus grew angry that his orders were not obeyed.

Around this time, a young professor of astronomy and mathematics entered Copernicus's life. He was Georg Joachim Rheticus (1514–1574), a professor of astrology, mathematics, and astronomy at the

University of Wittenberg in Germany. In 1538, Rheticus left Wittenberg in the hope of learning astronomy from Copernicus. Rheticus wrote:

> *I heard of the fame of Master Nicolaus Copernicus in the northern lands, and although the University of Wittenberg had made me a Public Professor in those arts, nonetheless, I did not think that I should be content until I had learned something more through the instruction of that man. … it seems to me that there came a great reward for these troubles, namely, that I, a rather daring young man, compelled this venerable man to share his ideas sooner in this discipline with the whole world.*

Rheticus arrived in Frombork in the spring of 1539. For the next two years, he worked with and learned from Copernicus. He was an able, willing and enthusiastic student.

One of the first tasks he took on was to read *On the Revolutions*, which had been gathering dust in Copernicus's home for more than nine years. After reading the work, Rheticus tried to persuade Copernicus to publish his book. He wrote a small booklet entitled *Narratio Primo*, or the *First Narration*, about Copernicus's theory, summarizing the ideas found in *On the Revolutions*. Rheticus believed that Copernicus had received inspiration directly from God. He said:

> *And so God gave the unlimited kingdom of Astronomy to the great scientist, the Doctor, my Teacher, because the lord thought it was appropriate to govern, administer, and increase the restoration of the Astronomical truth.*

Rheticus believed God gave the key to all astronomy to Copernicus because he saw that Copernicus was a great scientist. Rheticus's booklet helped attract attention to Copernicus's new ideas and spark public interest in the book's upcoming publication.

Before the book went to the printer, Copernicus wrote a preface to Pope Paul III, who had a reputation as a scholar. He tried to explain his work:

> *I can easily conceive, most Holy Father, that as soon as some people learn that in this book which I have written concerning the revolutions of the heavenly bodies, I ascribe certain motions to the Earth, they will cry out at once that I and my theory should be rejected.*

Despite the crucial role Rheticus played in bringing Copernicus's book to completion, the first edition of On the Revolutions does not mention Rheticus anywhere by name. Although he thanked his many friends for encouraging him to publish his book, Copernicus only names officials of the Roman Catholic Church who supported its publication.

On the Revolutions *was written in Latin, the language of science and the church.*

AD LECTOREM DE HYPO-
THESIBVS HVIVS OPERIS.

NON dubito, quin eruditi quidam, uulgata iam de nouitate hypotheſeon huius operis fama, quòd terram mobilem, Solem uero in medio uniuerſi immobilẽ conſtituit, uehementer ſint offenſi, puténtq; diſciplinas liberales rectè iam olim conſtitutas, turbari nõ oportere. Verum ſi rem exactè perpendere uolent, inueniẽt authorem huius operis, nihil quod reprehendi mereatur cõmiſiſſe. Eſt enim Aſtronomi proprium, hiſtoriam motuum cœleſtium diligenti & artificioſa obſeruatione colligere. Deinde cauſas earundem, ſeu hypotheſes, cum ueras aſſequi nulla ratione poſſit, qualeſcunq; excogitare & confingere, quibus ſuppoſitis, ijdem motus, ex Geometriæ principijs, tam in futurũ, quàm in præteritũ rectè poſſint calculari. Horũ autẽ utrunq; egregie præſtitit hic artifex. Neq; enim neceſſe eſt, eas hypotheſes eſſe ueras, imò ne ueriſimiles quidem, ſed ſufficit hoc unum, ſi calculum obſeruationibus congruentem exhibeant. niſi fortè quis Geometriæ & Optices uſq;adeo ſit ignarus, ut epicyclium Veneris pro ueriſimili habeat, ſeu in cauſa eſſe credat, quod ea quadraginta partibus, & eo amplius, Solẽ interdum præcedat, interdũ ſequatur. Quis enim nõ uidet, hoc poſito, neceſſario ſequi, diametrum ſtellæ in περιγείῳ pluſq; quadruplo, corpus autem ipſum pluſq; ſedecuplo, maiora, quàm in ἀπογείῳ apparere, cui tamen omnis æui experientia refragatur? Sunt & alia in hac diſciplina non minus abſurda, quæ in præſentiarum excutere, nihil eſt neceſſe. Satis enim patet, apparentiũ inæqualium motuũ cauſas, hanc artẽ penitus & ſimpliciter ignorare. Et ſi quas fingẽdo excogitat, ut certe quãplurimas excogitat, nequaquã tamen in hoc excogitat, ut ita eſſe cuiquam perſuadeat, ſed tantum, ut calculum rectè inſtituant. Cum autem unus & eiuſdem motus, uarie interdum hypotheſes ſeſe offerant (ut in motu Solis, eccentricitas, & epicyclium) Aſtronomus eam potiſsimum arripiet, quæ compræhenſu ſit quàm facillima, Philoſophus fortaſſe, ueri ſimilitudinem magis re-

Copernicus, who expected people to scorn his theory, wrote:

> *Perhaps there will be babblers who, although completely ignorant of mathematics, nevertheless take it upon themselves to pass judgment on mathematical questions and … will dare find fault with my undertaking and censure [condemn] it.*

Rheticus took Copernicus's book to Nuremberg, Germany, to be printed. A printer had to hand-set the type based on the handwritten manuscript. This was neither a quick nor an easy process. Rheticus left an editor, Andreas Osiander, in charge of overseeing the actual printing. To the preface Copernicus had written, Osiander added one of his own. The Osiander preface states:

> *Therefore, alongside the ancient hypotheses [ideas], which are no more probable, let us permit these new hypotheses also to become known. … Let no one expect anything certain from astronomy, which can not furnish it, lest he accept as the truth ideas conceived for another purpose, and depart from this study a greater fool than when he entered it.*

In short, Osiander instructed readers to take Copernicus's theory only as a highly questionable hypothesis. It was a common tactic in astronomy to prevent controversy by identifying new models as hypotheses rather than as truths. However, since Osiander did not sign his preface, many readers believed that Copernicus wrote Osiander's words. In other words,

Andreas Osiander did not sign his preface to Copernicus's book because as a Lutheran, signing his name would have suggested that Protestants sympathized with Copernicus's views. Lutherans already had a major role since they were publishing the book.

readers actually thought that Copernicus did not believe in his own work.

The printer produced nearly 500 copies of *On the Revolutions* in March 1543. The book sold for the equivalent of $200 in present-day U.S. currency. For most people living in 1543, that was more than a year's wages.

While the book was readied for the press, Copernicus's health began to fail. He had enjoyed good health most of his life, but in early 1543, he had a stroke, which left him partially paralyzed on his right side. His memory was failing, and he lost the desire to live. Eventually, he slipped into a coma.

Although the book was printed in March, Copernicus did not receive a copy until the day he died, May 24, 1543. According to legend, he was roused briefly from his coma to hold a copy of *On the Revolutions* just before he died. According to his friend Tiedemann Giese:

> *[Copernicus's death] was caused by a hemorrhage and subsequent paralysis of the right side on 24 May, his memory and mental alertness having been lost many days before. He saw his treatise [book] only at his last breath on his dying day.*

Copernicus was buried in the Cathedral of Warmia, Poland. He had no wife or children, and he

On his deathbed, Copernicus finally saw the fruits of his life's work.

left just over 71 marks to each of his niece's seven children. Copernicus owned nearly three dozen books, which he left to the library at Heilsberg, Germany, and to a physician friend. His library contained copies of the *Alfonsine Tables*, Ptolemy's

Cosmographia, and Euclid's *Elementa*. Today, any one book from Copernicus's library would be worth millions of dollars.

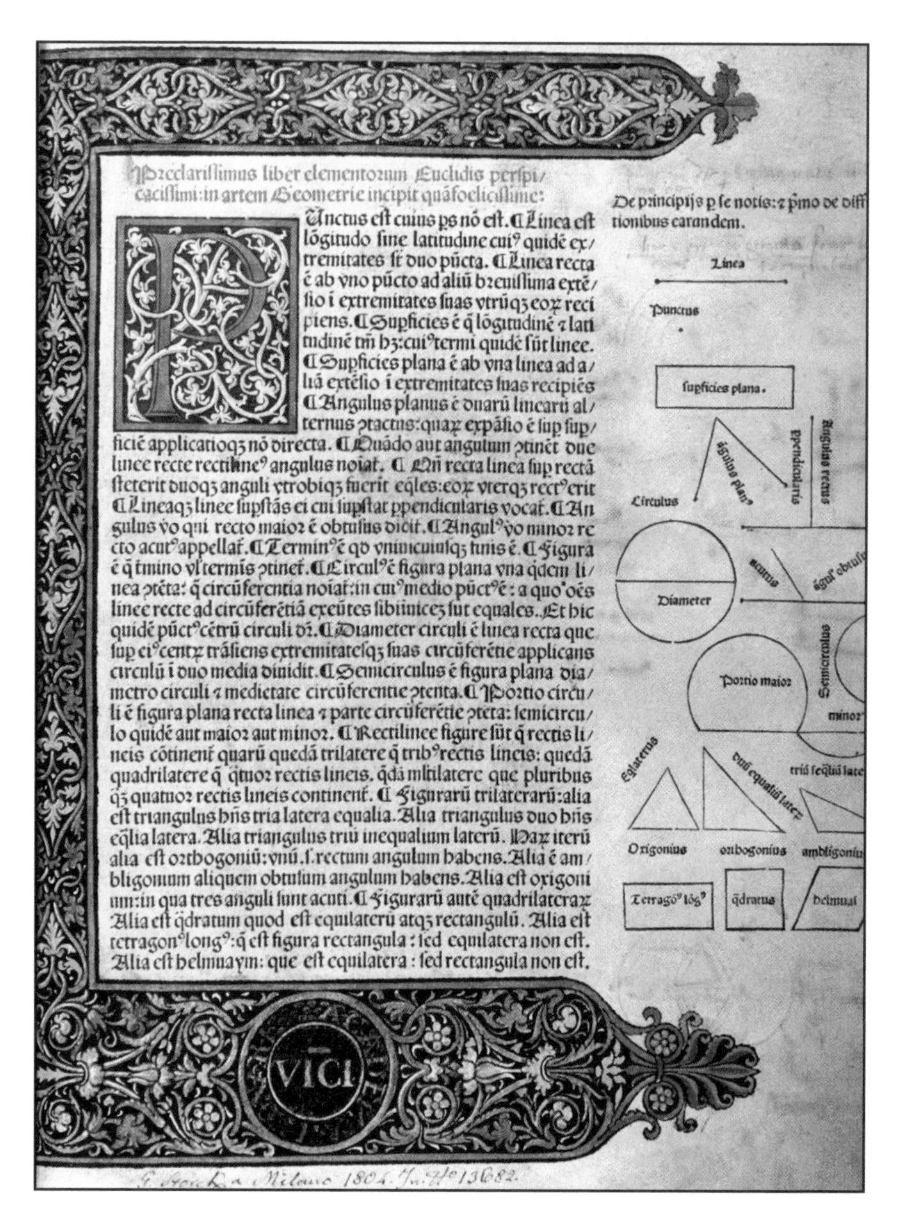
Preclarissimus liber elementorum Euclidis perspi/
cacissimi: in artem Geometrie incipit quãfoelicissime:

Punctus est cuius ps nõ est. ¶ Linea est
lõgitudo sine latitudine cuiꝰ quidẽ ex/
tremitates sũt duo pũcta. ¶ Linea recta
ẽ ab vno pũcto ad aliũ breuissima extẽ/
sio i extremitates suas vtrũq3 eoꝝ reci
piens. ¶ Supficies ẽ q̃ lõgitudinẽ & lati
tudinẽ tm̃ h3: cuiꝰ termi quidẽ sũt linee.
¶ Supficies plana ẽ ab vna linea ad a/
liã extẽsio i extremitates suas recipiẽs
¶ Angulus planus ẽ duarũ linearũ al/
ternus ɔtactus: quaꝝ expãsio ẽ sup sup/
ficiẽ applicatioq3 nõ directa. ¶ Quãdo aut angulum ɔtinẽt due
linee recte rectilineꝰ angulus noiat. ¶ Qñ recta linea sup rectã
steterit duoq3 anguli vtrobiq3 fuerit eq̃les: eoꝝ vterq3 rectꝰ erit
¶ Lineaq3 linee supstãs ei cui supstat ppendicularis vocat. ¶ An
gulus vo qui recto maior ẽ obtusus dicit. ¶ Angulꝰ vo minor re
cto acutꝰ appellat. ¶ Terminꝰ ẽ qd vniuscuiusq3 finis ẽ. ¶ Figura
ẽ q̃ tmino vl termis ɔtinet. ¶ Circulꝰ ẽ figura plana vna q̃dem li/
nea ɔtẽta: q̃ circũferentia noiat: in cuiꝰ medio pũctꝰ ẽ: a quo oẽs
linee recte ad circũferẽtiã exeũtes sibiinice3 sut equales. Et hic
quidẽ pũctꝰ cẽtrũ circuli dr. ¶ Diameter circuli ẽ linea recta que
sup eiꝰ centꝝ trãsiens extremitatesq3 suas circũferẽtie applicans
circulũ i duo media diuidit. ¶ Semicirculus ẽ figura plana dia/
metro circuli & medietate circũferentie ɔtenta. ¶ Portio circu/
li ẽ figura plana recta linea & parte circũferẽtie ɔteta: semicircu/
lo quidẽ aut maior aut minor. ¶ Rectilinee figure sũt q̃ rectis li/
neis cõtinent quarũ quedã trilatere q̃ tribꝰ rectis lineis: quedã
quadrilatere q̃ q̃tuor rectis lineis. q̃dã mltilatere que pluribus
q3 quatuor rectis lineis continent. ¶ Figurarũ trilaterarũ: alia
est triangulus hñs tria latera equalia. Alia triangulus duo hñs
eq̃lia latera. Alia triangulus triũ inequalium laterũ. Haꝝ iterũ
alia est orthogoniũ: vnũ .s. rectum angulum habens. Alia ẽ am/
bligonium aliquem obtusum angulum habens. Alia est oxigoni
um: in qua tres anguli sunt acuti. ¶ Figurarũ autẽ quadrilateraꝝ
Alia est q̃dratum quod est equilaterũ atq3 rectangulũ. Alia est
tetragonꝰ longꝰ: q̃ est figura rectangula: sed equilatera non est.
Alia est helmuaym: que est equilatera: sed rectangula non est.

De principijs p se notis: & pmo de diffi
tionibus earundem.

A late 15th-century copy of Euclid's Elementa is beautifully illustrated.

After Copernicus's *On the Revolutions* was published, many things stood in the way of its success. There were few books and no way of circulating them. Hardly anyone could afford the book, and few people could read it. Although the view it proposed would not be adopted by the world for some time, *On the Revolutions* was studied seriously by members of the scientific community from the moment of its publication. Scholars began to read, believe, and talk about Copernicus's ideas. Earth was not the center of the universe, and man was not the focal point of the world.

A Scientific Revolution

The Renaissance brought about a scientific revolution that happened over more than a century. It took time to make people give up old ways of thinking and accept new ideas. Copernicus and his work were part of this revolution.

Many events caused the scientific revolution. First, expanded trade and travel brought different thoughts and knowledge to Europe. In particular, the science and medicine of the Islamic and Chinese worlds offered plenty for Europeans to consider. In addition, European universities began to expand the courses they offered. Professors were no longer limited by the strict viewpoints of the Roman Catholic Church.

This scientific revolution also grew because of

A statue in Montreal, Canada, honors Nicolaus Copernicus.

the invention of movable type in 1455. Johannes Gutenberg's printing press made producing books quicker and cheaper. Although printed books still cost the equivalent of $200, they were nevertheless available, and some people did buy them.

The Protestant Reformation added to the acceptance of new views toward science and learning. People began to question some of the old beliefs and outdated science and pursue new science.

To counter the growth of the Protestant movement, the Roman Catholic Church held the Council of Trent from 1545 to 1563, which set up standards for the moral behavior of Catholics. It was strongly anti-Protestant and added stricter, harsher rules for Catholics to follow. The council also created the *Index of Prohibited Books*, a list of banned books that did not present the church's established thoughts or values. The church believed that if it stopped Catholics from reading material that disagreed with its policies and beliefs, people would not accept "wrong" thinking. The church took a hard look at anyone who stepped out of line. Those who did not follow the strict church rules were labeled heretics—and convicted heretics were executed.

For many years after Copernicus died, the Roman Catholic Church was not concerned with his book. The first indication of possible trouble came from Giordano Bruno, an Italian with some new and challenging ideas.

Bruno was a Dominican priest who devoted himself to study and travel. Unfortunately for the church, Bruno chose to study magic, and had a strong interest in Egyptian, Hebrew, and Greek magic. He was an outspoken supporter of Copernicus's theories, although his understanding of the astronomer's work was flawed. Bruno had no training in mathematical astronomy and misunderstood basic aspects of Copernicus's model, so although he was associated with its support, he was not a very credible spokesman for the Copernican system.

Furthermore, Bruno offered additional theories of the universe that challenged the church's position far beyond Copernicus's sun-centered model. Bruno theorized that the Holy Spirit was a living being and that the universe had no bounds.

Giordano Bruno (1548–1600)

Church officials arrested Bruno for heresy and put him in jail for eight years. When he refused to change his thinking, they ordered him to be burned at the stake. Because Bruno's questionable ideas went so far beyond those Copernicus had described, the church did not address the Copernicus situation at that time.

At the same time, Danish scientist Tycho Brahe was becoming interested in Copernicus's theories. Brahe served as the Danish royal astrologer. At that time, most astronomers made their living by serving

Tycho Brahe (1546–1601)

as astrologers to wealthy or noble families. Brahe set up an observatory on the island of Hveen, about 20 miles (32 kilometers) from Copenhagen, Denmark. Brahe created new standards for observing the stars and planets without a telescope. He built very accurate instruments for astronomical observations with the naked eye.

Based on his own observations, Brahe theorized that the planets orbited the sun, but the sun and moon orbited Earth. Brahe had excellent instruments, but he drew faulty conclusions from the data he collected.

Then Brahe received a remarkable gift—the "rulers of Ptolemy" that had been built by Copernicus. This was Copernicus's 8-foot (2.4-m) long triquetrum. Brahe was thrilled to have something once owned by the great scientist Copernicus. He wrote a poem showing his enthusiasm at receiving Copernicus's triquetrum:

> *He [Copernicus] was like no men, by the Earth for several centuries*
> *Procreated, like the bests who come without rushes*
> *The Stars themselves barely bore through thousand comebacks,*
> *And although they so quickly move their orbs in tracks And by so much centers, poles, circles, never tired, never quieten*
> *He who was engendered by the heaven,*

engendered for the earthmen,
The celestial bodies ...

Brahe compared the star tables Copernicus had created to the *Alfonsine Tables*. He found that Copernicus calculated more accurate results. In 1574, Brahe spoke at the University of Copenhagen:

> *Through observations made by himself, he [Copernicus] discovered certain gaps in Ptolemy ... he found the Alfonsine computations in disagreement with the motions of the heavens. ... He restored the science of the heavenly motions in such a way that nobody before him reasoned more accurately about the movements of the heavenly bodies.*

While Brahe made a modest impact on the scientific world, one of his students became a beacon for scientific advancement. His name was Johannes Kepler, a German who studied mathematics and astronomy at the University of Tübingen, Germany. Kepler became Brahe's assistant and studied Brahe's records of his observations. Based on Brahe's records, Kepler decided that orbits were actually ellipses, not the perfect circles that Copernicus had proposed.

Kepler developed three laws of planetary motion that corrected some of Copernicus's errors. These laws are accepted today as accurate models for the movement of planets. Kepler's first law is the law of elliptical orbits. Simply stated, planets move around the sun in an elliptical pattern, which looks similar to an oval.

The second law is the law of areas. This law stated that an imaginary line connecting any planet to the sun sweeps over equal areas in equal intervals of time. Suppose a line is drawn from Mars to the sun. During a 24-hour period, the line moves along the orbit. It marks a section shaped like a piece of pie. Now, suppose a line is drawn from Jupiter to the sun. The line is much longer, but during one 24-hour period, it marks a section equal in area to the section cut by Mars. One is a short, fatter slice, and the other is longer and thinner. Both cover equal areas.

Johannes Kepler (1571–1630)

Kepler's third law is the harmonic law, which involves higher math. The time a planet takes to make a complete orbit around the sun is called a period. The earth's period equals one year. Kepler's law says that the square of the period of any planet is in proportion to the cube of its mean distance from the sun. In other words, the farther away from the sun a planet is found, the larger will be its orbit.

Although the laws corrected several of Copernicus's ideas, Kepler did agree that the planets revolved around the sun. Kepler followed Brahe's lead in discounting the church's view of the universe and accepting Copernicus's heliocentric theory.

While Kepler studied the heavens in northern Europe, another astronomer of note—Galileo Galilei—did so from Italy. Kepler worked far from the powerful influence of the Roman Catholic Church. Galileo lived nearer to the heart of the church's power, and he suffered for it.

Galileo was born in Pisa, Italy, and studied in Padua, Italy. He was an astronomer and mathematician, like Copernicus and Kepler. Unlike Copernicus, Galileo had the advantage of using a new scientific instrument—the telescope. He saw craters in the moon and sun spots bursting from the sun. He linked astronomy with the motion of Earth. His observations supported Copernicus's sun-centered ideas, and it got him in trouble. In a letter to Kepler dated August 4, 1597, Galileo wrote:

> *Many years ago, I accepted Copernicus' theory, and from that point of view, I*

discovered the reasons for numerous natural phenomena. ... I have not dared to publish up to now. For I am thoroughly frightened by what happened to our master, Copernicus. ... Among countless (for so large is the number of fools) he became a target for ridicule and derision.

Galileo had good reason to be afraid. At first, the church ignored Galileo's observations, but then

Galileo Galilei (1564–1642)

Galileo's work seemed to support Copernican ideas, challenging the church's interpretation of the Bible. The Bible says in a number of places that the sun moves and Earth stays still. Galileo questioned whether the Bible should be interpreted scientifically, reasoning that the Bible was meant to tell us "how to go to heaven, not how the heavens go."

In 1616, the Roman Catholic Church officially forbade the study of Copernicus's ideas. They suggested "corrections" to *On the Revolutions* and placed the book on the *Index of Prohibited Books* until the corrections were made. The changes removed all mention that a sun-centered universe or that Earth's motion could actually be demonstrated. For example, one change inserted the word *hypothesis* to change "Demonstration of the motion of the Earth" to "Demonstration of the hypothesis of the motion of the Earth." Once the changes were made, Copernicus's book could be read again. Unfortunately for Galileo, he had read the original and believed it to be true.

In 1633, the church arrested Galileo and tried him for suspicion of heresy. He had to say that he no longer agreed with Copernicus and that the church's teachings were correct. In June 1663, he wrote:

> *I, Galileo, son of the late Vincenzio Galilei of Florence, seventy years of age, … kneel-*

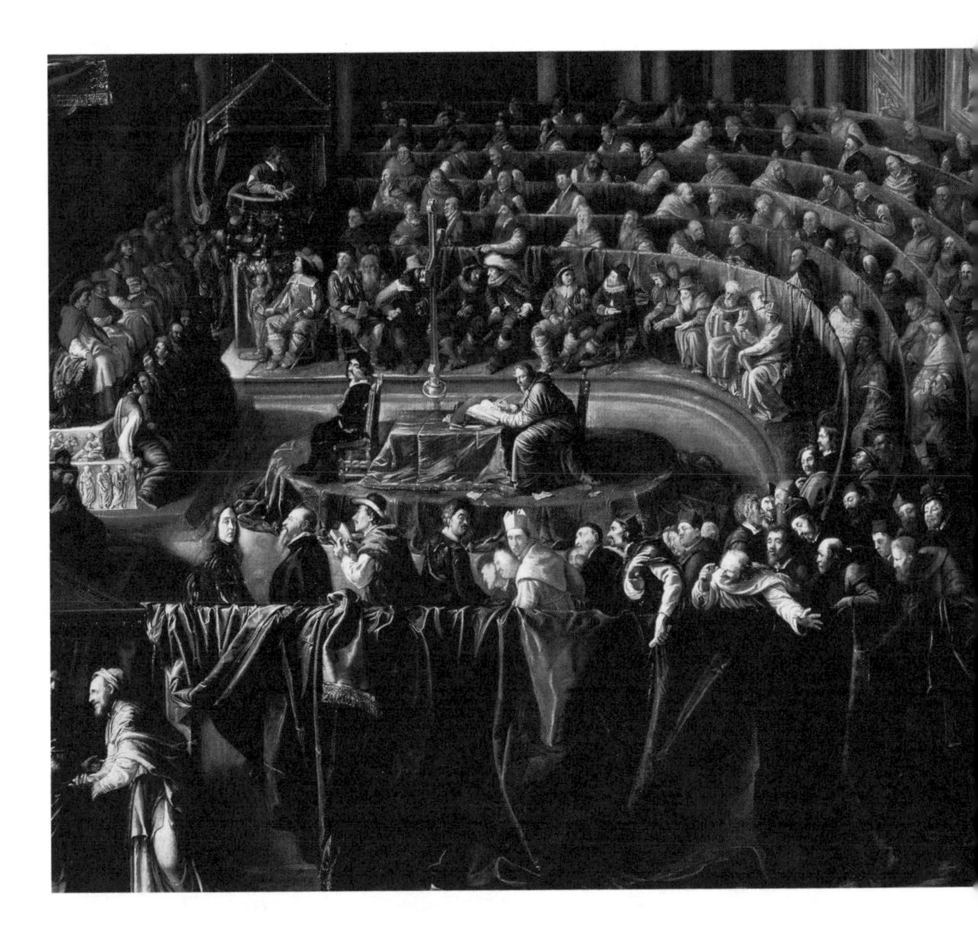

ing before you Most Eminent and Most Reverent Cardinals ... swear that I have always believed, I believe now, and with God's help I will believe in the future all that the Holy Catholic and Apostolic Church holds, preaches, and teaches. ... [I will] abandon completely the false opinion that the sun is the center of the world and does not move and the earth is not the center of the world and moves.

In 1633, Galileo stood trial before the Inquisition, an effort by the Roman Catholic Church to find and punish heretics.

The church brought Galileo to his knees in repentance, and the scientist lived his remaining years under house arrest.

For more than 200 years, the Roman Catholic Church kept the works of Copernicus, Kepler, and Galileo on its list of banned books. That didn't mean they weren't read, however. Scientists and free-thinkers read them and learned the new science. In 1835, Copernicus's *On the Revolutions* was finally removed from the *Index of Prohibited Books*, and in 1992, the church finally admitted it had been a too harsh on Galileo.

A large crater on the moon, seen on the horizon in the lower right corner of this photo, was named after Nicolaus Copernicus.

Twenty years earlier, the National Aeronautics and Space Administration's *Apollo 17* mission to the moon took pictures of a large, round crater, which was later named for Copernicus. Between 1972 and 1981, NASA launched its third orbiting astronomical observatory. This satellite, named *Copernicus*, was launched to find answers to some basic questions about the stars. The *Copernicus* scanned the heavens for new, exciting information—much as its namesake did more than 400 years earlier.

Today, Nicolaus Copernicus is considered the father of modern astronomy. Not all his ideas were correct, and not all his computations were accurate. But, he did offer a new—and, at the time, strange—view of the universe. He made people think, and in doing so, he changed their ideas. He started a revolution in astronomy that continues to this day. Copernicus turned all eyes toward the sky, to a universe of moving planets and distant stars.

Copernicus's Life

1473
Born February 19 in Torún, Poland

1483
Copernicus's father dies; his uncle, Bishop Lucas Watzenrode, is named guardian

1480

1474
Isabella becomes queen of Aragon; known as the "First Lady of the Renaissance"

1485
Henry VII is crowned king of England, beginning the 117-year reign of England's Tudor dynasty

World Events

1491

Begins studies at the University of Kraków, Poland; assumes Latin spelling of his name

1496

Studies canon law at the University of Bologna, Italy

1495

1492

Ferdinand and Isabella of Spain finance the voyage of the Italian Christopher Columbus to the New World

Copernicus's Life

1497

Assumes the job of canon in Frombork, Poland, but continues university studies

1500

Observes a lunar eclipse

1500

World Events

1497

Vasco da Gama becomes the first western European to find a sea route to India

1503

Receives a degree in canon law from the University of Ferrara, Italy

1507

Becomes the private physician of his uncle; works on his short book *Commentariolis*

1510–1512

Draws a map of Warmia, Poland

1510

1509

Henry, the prince of Wales, becomes King Henry VIII of England at age 18

1513

Vasco Nuñez de Balboa is the first European to reach the Pacific Ocean

Copernicus's Life

1516

Assists Pope Leo X in revising the calendar

1521

Assists in rebuilding Frombork after it is burned by the Knights of the Teutonic Order

1520

1517

Martin Luther posts his *95 Theses* on the door of the Palast Church in Wittenberg, beginning the Protestant Reformation in Germany

1524

German peasants rise up against their landlords in The Peasant's War, the greatest mass uprising in German history

World Events

1530

Finishes major writing of *On the Revolutions of the Heavenly Spheres*

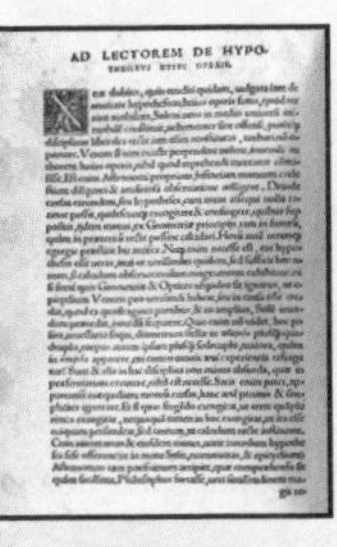

AD LECTOREM DE HYPO-

1543

On the Revolutions of the Heavenly Spheres is published; dies in Frombork on May 24

1540

1531

The "great comet," later called Halley's Comet, causes a wave of superstition

1535

The first complete English translation of the Bible is printed in Germany

Life at a Glance

Full name:	Nicolaus Copernicus
Alternate Spellings:	Mikolaj Kopernik, Nicolaus Koppernigk
Date of Birth:	February 18, 1473
Birthplace:	Torún, Poland
Father:	Nicolaus Koppernigk
Mother:	Barbara Watzenrode Koppernigk
Education:	University of Kraków (1491–1494), liberal arts and astronomy
	University of Bologna (1496–1500), canon law
	University of Padua (1501–1503), medicine
	University of Ferrara (1503), Doctor of Canon Law
Date of Death:	May 24, 1543
Place of Burial:	Frombork, Poland

In the Library

Andronik, Catherine M. *Copernicus: Founder of Modern Astronomy.* Berkeley Heights, N.J.: Enslow Publishers, Inc., 2002.

Goble, Todd. *Nicholas Copernicus and the Founding of Modern Astronomy.* Greensboro, N.C.: Morgan Reynolds Publishing, Inc., 2004.

Henbest, Nigel. *Spotters Guide to the Night Sky.* London: Usborne Books, 2000.

Lippincott, Kristen. *Eyewitness: Astronomy.* New York: DK Publishing, 1999.

Look for more Signature Lives books about this era:

Christopher Columbus: *Explorer of the New World*
ISBN 0-7565-1811-8

Elizabeth I: *Queen of Tudor England*
ISBN 0-7565-0988-2

Galileo: *Astronomer and Physicist*
ISBN 0-7565-0813-4

Johannes Gutenberg: *Inventor of the Printing Press*
ISBN 0-7565-0989-0

Michelangelo: *Sculptor and Painter*
ISBN 0-7565-0814-2

Francisco Pizarro: *Conqueror of the Incas*
ISBN 0-7565-0815-0

William Shakespeare: *Playwright and Poet*
ISBN 0-7565-0816-9

Additional Resources

On the Web

For more information on *Nicolaus Copernicus*, use FactHound to track down Web sites related to this book.

1. Go to *www.facthound.com*
2. Type in a search word related to this book or this book ID: 0756508126
3. Click on the *Fetch It* button.

FactHound will find the best Web sites for you.

Historic Sites

Lakeview Museum of the Arts and Sciences
1125 W. Lake Ave.
Peoria, IL 61614
309/686-7000
To see the world's largest scale model of the universe

Smithsonian National Air and Space Museum
Independence Avenue at Fourth Street Southwest
Washington, DC 20560
202/633-1000
To learn more about the discoveries of Copernicus and other astronomers

astronomy
the science of studying stars, planets, and other heavenly bodies

axis
a real or imaginary line passing through the middle of an object around which the object rotates

canon
a man who served the church but was not a priest

ducats
gold coins issued by Rome

heliocentric
centered on the sun

heretic
a person who speaks out against a church's established beliefs

hypothesis
something that is suggested as being true for the purpose of further study

latitude
an imaginary line running east to west on a globe that establishes distance from the north or south pole

observatory
a place or building set up for studying the stars, sun, moon, and planets

orbit
the invisible path followed by an object circling a planet, the sun, or other heavenly body

perpendicular
straight up and down

theory
a proposed explanation for an idea or belief

Chapter 1

Page 13, line 3: Peter Landry. "Biographies: Nicolaus Copernicus (1473–1543)." Biographies. www.blupete.com/Literature/Biographies/Science/Copernicus.htm

Chapter 3

Page 30, line 5: Jan Adamczewski. *Nicolaus Copernicus and his Epoch.* Philadelphia: Copernicus Society of America, 1972, p. 92.

Chapter 4

Page 35, line 8: Andrew White. "Astronomy: The Warfare of Science with Theology." http://www.infidels.org/library/historical/andrew_white/Chapter3.html

Page 36, line 3: Owen Gingrich. *The Eye of Heaven: Ptolemy, Copernicus, Kepler.* New York: American Institute of Physics, 1993, p. 163.

Page 42, line 2: Pierre Gassendi and Olivier Thill. *The Life of Copernicus: The Man Who Did Not Change the World.* Fairfax, Va.: Xulon Press, 2002, p. 165.

Page 45, line 3: *Nicolaus Copernicus and his Epoch*, p. 133.

Chapter 5

Page 52, line 5: Nicolaus Copernicus. *On the Revolutions of the Celestial Spheres.* (C. G. Wallis, trans.) In *Great Books of the Western World, Vol. 15.* Chicago: Encyclopedia Britannica, 1990, p. 507.

Chapter 6

Page 63, line 8: Nicolaus Copernicus. *On the Revolutions of the Celestial Spheres.* (Edward Rosen, trans.) Baltimore, Md.: The Johns Hopkins University Press, 1992, p. xix.

Page 63, line 24: John Henry. *Moving Heaven and Earth: Copernicus and the Solar System.* Cambridge, England: Icon Books, Ltd., 2001, pp. 52–53.

Page 64, line 8: *On the Revolutions of the Celestial Spheres.* (Rosen), p. 8.

Page 64, line 21: "Copernicus: Cleric and Astronomer." LucidCafe Library. www.lucidcafe.com/library/96feb/copernicus.html

Page 67, sidebar: *On the Revolutions of the Celestial Spheres* (Rosen), book I, chapter 10.

Page 68, line 14: Herman Kesten. *Copernicus and His World.* (E. B. Ashton and Norbert Gutterman, trans.) New York: Roy Publishing Co., 1945, p. vii.

Chapter 7

Page 74, line 4: J.J. O'Connor and E.F. Robertson. "Georg Joachim von Lauchen Rheticus." School of Mathematics and Statistics, University of St. Andrew's, Scotland. www-gap.dcs.st-and.ac.uk/~history/Mathematicians/Rheticus.html

Page 75, line 2: *The Life of Copernicus: The Man Who Did Not Change the World*, pp. 185–186.

Page 75, line 19: Nicolaus Copernicus. *On the Revolutions of the Celestial Spheres.* (Rosen), preface.

Page 76, line 3: J.J. O'Connor and E.F. Robertson. "Nicolaus Copernicus." School of Mathematics and Statistics, University of St. Andrew's, Scotland. www-gap.dcs.st-and.ac.uk/~history/Mathematicians/Copernicus.html

Page 77, line 9: "The Scandal of the Osiander Preface." http://condor.stcloudstate.edu/~physcrse/astr106/ossiander.html

Page 78, line 20: *The Life of Copernicus: The Man Who Did Not Change the World*, p. 226.

Chapter 8

Page 87, line 20: Ibid., p. 245.

Page 88, line 7: Ibid., p. 247.

Page 90, line 26: Ibid., pp. 285–286.

Page 92, line 6: *Moving Heaven and Earth: Copernicus and the Solar System*, p. 95.

Page 92, line 26: Giorgio de Santillana. *The Crime of Galileo.* Chicago: University of Chicago Press, 1955 pp. 310—311.

Select Bibliography

Adamczewski, Jan. *Nicolaus Copernicus and his Epoch.* Philadelphia: Copernicus Society of America, 1972.

Andronik, Catherine M. *Copernicus: Founder of Modern Astronomy.* Berkeley Heights, N.J.: Enslow Publishers, Inc., 2002.

Copernicus, Nicolas. *On the Revolutions of the Celestial Spheres* (C. G. Wallis, trans.). In *Great Books of the Western World, Volume 15.* Chicago: Encyclopedia Britannica, 1990.

Copernicus, Nicolaus. *On the Revolutions of the Celestial Spheres* (Edward Rosen, trans). Baltimore, Md.: The Johns Hopkins University Press, 1992.

Gassendi, Pierre, and Olivier Thill. *The Life of Copernicus: The Man Who Did Not Change the World.* Fairfax, Va.: Xulon Press, 2002.

Gingrich, Owen. *The Book Nobody Read: Chasing the Revolutions of Nicolaus Copernicus.* New York: Walker & Company, 2004.

Gingrich, Owen. *The Eye of Heaven: Ptolemy, Copernicus. Kepler.* New York: American Institute of Physics, 1993.

Gingrich, Owen. *The Great Copernicus Chase and Other Adventures in Astronomical History.* Cambridge, Mass.: Sky Publishing Corporation, 1992.

Goble, Todd. *Nicholas Copernicus and the Founding of Modern Astronomy.* Greensboro, N.C.: Morgan Reynolds Publishing, Inc., 2004.

Henry, John. *Moving Heaven and Earth: Copernicus and the Solar System.* Cambridge, England: Icon Books, Ltd., 2001.

Hoyle, Fred. *Nicolaus Copernicus: An Essay on his Life and Work.* New York: Harper & Row, Publishers, 1973.

Kesten, Herman. *Copernicus and His World* (E. B. Ashton and Norbert Gutterman, trans.). New York: Roy Publishing Co., 1945.

Index

About the Author

Barbara A. Somervill has been writing for more than 30 years. She has written newspaper and magazine articles, video scripts, and books for children. She enjoys writing about science and investigating people's lives for biographies. She is an avid reader and traveler. Ms. Somervill lives with her husband in South Carolina.

Image Credits

Chris Lisle/Corbis, cover (top), 4–5; Paul Almasy/Corbis, cover (bottom), 2, 47, 73; Erich Lessing/Art Resource, N.Y., 8, 24, 34, 38, 45, 48, 55, 58, 89, 93, 100 (top); Bettmann/Corbis, 11, 20, 31, 53; M. ou Me. Desjeux, Bernard/Corbis, 14, 17, 96 (top); Jim Steinhart/PlanetWare, 22, 97 (top); Mary Evans Picture Library, 29, 79, 98 (top), 101 (top right); Roger Ressmeyer/Corbis, 29 (inset); Stock Montage/Getty Images, 32, 99 (top); Image Select/Art Resource, N.Y., 36; Scala/Art Resource, N.Y., 41, 91; Foto Marburg/Art Resource, N.Y., 43; SEF/Art Resource, N.Y., 50; North Wind Picture Archives, 57, 70; Stapleton Collection/Corbis, 60; Hulton/Archive by Getty Images, 62, 85; Marilyn Moseley LaMantia, 65; Stefano Bianchetti/Corbis, 66; Courtesy History of Science Collections, University of Oklahoma Libraries, 76, 80, 101 (top left); Carl & Ann Purcell/Corbis, 82; Kean Collection/Getty Images, 86; NASA/Corbis, 94; Library of Congress, 96 (bottom), 97 (bottom), 98 (bottom), 99 (bottom), 100 (bottom); PhotoDisc, 101 (bottom).